read without prejudice
GEORGE**MICHAEL**

PHOTOGRAPHIC CREDITS

© ALL ACTION

© PICTORIAL PRESS

© REDFERNS

© REX FEATURES

Copyright © 1997 UFO MUSIC LTD

All rights reserved. Printed in Great Britain. No part of this book may be used or reproduced in any manner whatsoever without written permission except in the case of brief quotations embodied in critical articles or reviews.

UFO Music Ltd 18 Hanway Street London W1P 9DD England
Telephone 0171 636 1281   Fax 0171 636 0738

First published in Great Britain 1997
UFO Music Ltd 18 Hanway Street
London W1P 9DD

The author and publishers have made every effort to contact all copyright holders. Any who for any reason have not been contacted are invited to write to the publishers so that a full acknowledgment may be made in subsequent editions of this work.

ISBN 1-873884-92-3

Designed by UFO Music Ltd

read without prejudice
GEORGE MICHAEL

Graham Betts

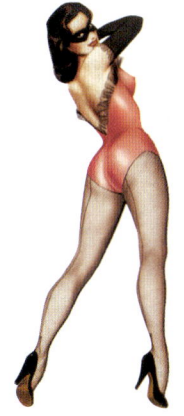

Enjoy what you do

CHAPTER ONE

In many ways, George Michael has defied the odds. Of the many groups who were operative at the same time his first outfit, Wham!, were enjoying their chart heyday, few remain in the listings on a regular basis. At the same time, solo artists emerging from within the confines of a group and going on to enjoy equal, let alone greater success than the act they started out with are even fewer on the ground. George Michael has been both the exception and exceptional. He was born on 25 June 1963 (his real name is Georgios Kyriacos Panayiotou) in Finchley, North London. Together with his two sisters Melanie and Yioda, he spent his childhood years living close to London, growing up in suburbs and offshoots such as Finchley, Burnt Oak and Radlett. And while he met and made many a childhood friend, none were to prove as lasting or important as the one he made on the first day of term in September 1975.

George was a first year pupil at Bushey Mead Comprehensive, and sat next to him on that first day was Andrew Ridgeley (born in Windlesham, Surrey on 26 January 1963). *"When I was about nine, I realised that I dominated the people I went around with,"* said George. *"Suddenly I realised that I didn't want to. I felt slightly unpleasant doing it. I completely changed and I remember thinking I'm not going to boss people about. Then I moved schools and met Andrew. He was the first friend I had that was as strong as me character wise, and that's why I didn't really need any others after that."*

Indeed, the pair clicked in a way only school colleagues can – and while most school acquaintances fall by the wayside the very minute they pass though the gates for the final time, this one proved longer-lasting. It helped, of course, that both George and Andrew shared an interest in music, following the fortunes of both Motown and the Specials' 2-Tone ska label in almost equal measure. So it was no surprise when, in 1979, George and Andrew linked up with Andrew's brother Paul, David Austin and Andrew Leaver to form the Executive, a ska-based group which secured a number of local gigs over the next 18 months but which hardly set the world alight.

The Executive called a halt in 1980 and George and Andrew spent much of the next two years concentrating on their songwriting and rehearsing (both 'Careless Whisper' and 'Club Tropicana', two future chartbusters, were written during this hiatus) and doing the kind of things most teenagers do: going to clubs and trying to find full-time employment. Of the two, George proved slightly more successful in obtaining work, although it was frequently part-time or casual and hardly the beginning of a career. **"I was a cinema usher and a builder's labourer,"** he'd later recall. **"There'd also been a Saturday job at British Home Stores, 'but I got the sack for not wearing a shirt and tie in the stock room. It was okay for Andrew to be on the dole because he was still living at home and he was a lazy bastard who just didn't want to go to work."** By January 1982, George and Andrew had managed to scrape together the £20 or so that was needed for the hire of a portable studio, they used it to record demo versions of four songs – 'Wham Rap', 'Come On!', 'Club Tropicana' and 'Careless Whisper' – which they then sent round to every major record company. **"What we wanted was for someone to give us £200 to do it in a studio,"** George now reveals. **"We were just looking for a chance to prove the songs. We went to music publishers at Virgin and about half a dozen other places and we used to turn up and pretend we had appointments. Otherwise they would never have agreed to see us."** The duo devised a devious routine to ensure they got a hearing. **"We would first be nice and then pretend that the secretary had made a mistake and get very angry – it really did work. We got into most of the big publishers that way, just turned up and did our routine. They nearly always believed you. They normally listened to the tape in our presence, usually they would turn it off after about ten or fifteen seconds. They used to tell us it was rubbish and send us away."**

CHAPTER ONE **ENJOY WHAT YOU DO**

If Wham! – as they were now christened, with an all-important exclamation mark – were expecting a flurry of A&R men (industry speak for talent scouts) knocking on their door, then they were to be bitterly disappointed, for not one of the major labels they touted their wares to expressed any interest whatsoever. Their luck changed slightly when they were introduced to former Phonogram employee Mark Dean, who had just set up his own Innervision company. Primarily a dance-orientated label, Innervision had one extra ace up its sleeve; a distribution deal with mighty CBS. The smaller label would ultimately score with Jimmy the Hoover, Animal Nightlife and of course Wham!, and on the strength of the demos he had heard Mark Dean was happy to offer Andrew and George a contract.

The group quickly returned to the studio to record their debut release, 'Wham Rap', with female recruits Shirlie Holliman and Mandy Washburn. At the same time, they signed a publishing deal with Morrison/Leahy Music Group whose co-founder, Dick Leahy, has since loomed large and long in the George Michael story.

Despite the marketing and promotional backing of CBS, 'Wham Rap' failed to chart in April 1982. To be fair there was considerable competition around at the time, with the likes of Bananarama, Simple Minds and Yazoo all charting for the first time. But, as George remembered, these first steps to fame were faltering ones indeed.

"Our very first PA was at a club called Level One in Neasden. And it was terrible because there were six hundred people in this club and, because there was no raised stage, they just formed a big circle around us. And so you are doing this thing and you have two really attractive girls with you, and you are trying to play out this little scenario between two couples – just like on Top Of The Pops **– but you had all the drunks coming up and joining in! And the drunks would go up behind the girls. It was an absolute nightmare."**

"Then we did Stringfellow's. I remember that was a really embarrassing one. I did this kick in the first routine and my shoe flew off into the crowd – so then I kicked the other one off with great aplomb to make it look deliberate! And I had to keep going. I was dancing in my socks on the glass floor of Stringfellow's and trying desperately not to cock it up, trying not to fall flat on my face. I was holding the fake mike with the fake lead and I remember going to the side of the dance floor with this thing and I felt the lead pull out, which totally exposed me as miming to the track." Undeterred, Wham! went back into the studio to record their second single 'Young Guns (Go For It)', with Diane Sealey (otherwise known as Dee C Lee) having replaced Mandy Washburn. Released in September 1982, 'Young Guns' proved to be an immediate hit with radio stations around the country, securing a place on numerous playlists. Sales proved a little slower, with the record finally hitting the Top 75 on 16 October and taking a month to rise into the Top 40. A coveted slot on *Top Of The Pops* proved to be the ultimate making of the record, for a memorable dance routine – shoes on, this time – helped to propel the record up to Number 3.

As 'Young Guns' began to slide back down the charts, the decision was taken to re-promote 'Wham Rap' as the next single. This time round it became a hit, aided by a club dance video, and made Number 8 in February 1983. The group had little time to bask in their success, for they were hard at work recording their debut album. Drafting in session musicians Deon Estus (bass), Robert Ahwai (guitar) and Anne Dudley (keyboards), 'Fantastic' began to take shape.

As well as the two hit singles already released, there would be a further two smashes ('Bad Boys' and 'Club Tropicana') and an interesting cover version of the Miracles' 'Love Machine' that would stand out from the album. And distinct areas of influence within the group were beginning to fall into line; George was responsible for the musical elements, penning most of the material and co-producing the album with Steve Brown, while Andrew was responsible for the style and image of the group.

George had already carefully considered how he wanted Wham! placed in the market place. 'We were out and out pop,' he confessed unashamedly. **"We thought it was the most honest thing to do. We didn't want to be subversive in any sense. We wanted to be huge stars. I knew I could do it. I knew that I had the capability, craft wise, to put us ahead of groups like Duran Duran and Culture Club, so I just went for it."**

That debut album was recorded against a backdrop of growing problems with Innervision. Indeed, by July 1983 Wham! were sufficiently distressed with their career to have consulted noted manager Simon Napier-Bell, hoping to find a possible escape route should the worst come to the worst. Meanwhile, there was still further single success to enjoy, as 'Bad Boys' proved to be one of the summer smashes of the year and peaked at Number 2. The accompanying video, shot in black and white and featuring George and Andrew in leather jackets, would be later described by George as one of the lowest points in the group's career. At the time, though, there was no doubt that the video proved to be an effective marketing tool in the development of Wham!

Their debut album was officially released on 2 July 1983 and seven days later distinguished itself by entering the UK chart at the very top. It was something of a remarkable debut, for not one of their singles had yet hit the summit. 'Fantastic' lasted just two weeks at Number 1 but would remain a chart regular for the next two years, finally bowing out after spending 116 weeks on the album chart. What made its chart longevity all the more surprising was that only one other single, the afore-mentioned 'Club Tropicana', was lifted as a single – and that peaked at 'only' Number 4.

"We've been slagged off for releasing it of course," George commented at the time 'Club Tropicana' took its bow on seven-inch plastic. **"It looks like we've gone more mainstream because we can do that now. The fact is that it's one of our oldest songs. Really, 'Wham Rap' drew us off course. Because we had so much press support then, we allowed ourselves to be swayed by it which we always said we wouldn't do. But it was a subconscious thing."**

"Although 'Young Guns' was a lot more mainstream," he continued, **"we still had the rap element and the social message in the anti-marriage lyric. With 'Bad Boys' we tried to get back to pop and when we realised how big our audience was getting, we thought it didn't matter about holding on to the club crowd. That's why we went back to 'Club Tropicana'."** Comment had also been made about the duo's physique and suntans, which they were far from embarrassed about showing off. **"Andrew and I couldn't have run about in shorts and done the video if we had been the colour of dead goldfishes,"** was how George justified it. **"Because there was something vaguely Mediterranean about us we were totally convincing when we went the 'Club Tropicana' route where two boys who were completely English wouldn't have been."** That August, George journeyed to the Muscle Shoals Studios in Alabama to work with legendary producer Jerry Wexler of Aretha Franklin fame on a solo version of 'Careless Whisper'. Although the sessions were an interesting lesson in production for the youngster, the final mix of the record was not to his liking and he decided against releasing the version he had been working on. Instead, the song would later be re-recorded with the assistance of Andy Richards in London.

George's first American venture was a disappointment all round, for Columbia had just released 'Bad Boys' in the US and the single peaked poorly at Number 60. The group's Stateside releases were all issued under the name of Wham! UK, for there was already another group recording for the GRT label who laid claim to the Wham title, although without ever hitting the Top 40. Despite their chart success at home, the autumn of 1983 was something of a tense time for Wham!, with Dee C Lee leaving the ranks to join Paul Weller's Style Council (she'd later marry her new 'boss'). She was eventually replaced by Pepsi Demacque. If the split with Lee had been amicable, the impending split with Mark Dean and Innervision was anything but. Wham!'s lawyer Tony Russell informed Dean in October that the group were looking to get out of their contract which was deemed to be highly restrictive. As he pondered the future implications for Innervision, Dean hastily assembled a mix of album tracks and released 'Club Fantastic Megamix' in November. Although the group were highly critical of the single and urged their growing fan base to ignore it, it still sold in sufficient quantities to hit Number 15.

Making it BIG

CHAPTER TWO

Matters were finally resolved the following March, with Wham! being switched to CBS's subsidiary Epic where they became labelmates with the Jacksons. George, meanwhile, was busy working on new songs for the group's second album. Although George would ultimately be credited with writing all of the material, Andrew could still provide inspiration; a note he left for his partner with the instruction 'wake me up before you go-go' would provide the group with their first chart topper.

Those early years spent listening to Motown obviously paid dividends for Wham!, for 'Wake Me Up Before You Go Go' was perhaps the biggest hit Motown never released. Instantly catchy and appealing, the single soon hit the top in the UK and spent two weeks at the summit, confirming George Michael as one of the better songwriters in action at the time. His craft and talent would also be appreciated in the US, where the single also topped the charts for three weeks and put the duo firmly on the map. **"I think 'Wake Me Up Before You Go Go' is undoubtedly the most remembered Wham! song because it is that much more stupid than anything else!"**, admitted the song's creator. **"I still look at that video and think it worked really perfectly for that song. Really poppy, really colourful – it totally captures that whole period. But although I see it working as a video, it makes me cringe for myself. But I was completely into the idea of being screamed at – I was very young and I can't pretend my ego didn't need that."** With their first Epic release at the top, George returned to the US, this time to Miami in order to film a video for the forthcoming solo release of 'Careless Whisper'. Released in July 1984, the song (co-written with Andrew a long time earlier) took barely three weeks to hit the top of the charts where it would remain for a similar period, selling over a million copies and in the process becoming Epic's first ever seven-figure seller).

George dedicated the single to his mother ('five minutes in return for 21 years') and watched in pleasure as the single topped the charts virtually all around the world over the next six months, including the US for three weeks. Its release in the US had born the legend Wham! featuring George Michael; it seemed a solo career was already being planned. And George was beginning to branch out into other areas, for 'Turn To Gold', a single he co-wrote and produced for David Austin, also featured on the UK charts.

The media were quick to latch onto the solo release, claiming it was the beginning of the end for Wham! as a group. But George would have none of it. 'No-one credits you with enough suss to develop two careers – one as a solo person and one with Wham!,' he explained. 'What's happening is this. As a solo artist, I want to go more towards soul. If I was left to my own devices, I'd probably try and sound like Marvin Gaye for the next five years. But the important thing is that together we make a pop group. **"We work better from a friendship that's built up over the last ten years. We're not Paul Newman and Steve McQueen** (that should of course read Paul Newman and Robert Redford!) **but it is like Butch Cassidy And The Sundance Kid – two blokes the same age who know each other back to front, upside down, inside out...giblets and all. There's a real strength there and we'll keep playing on that. Though it sounds calculated, we want to make sure people realise that all the time."** The hit run continued into October, with 'Freedom' becoming the group's third chart topper and heading the pile for three weeks. Its success was no doubt especially pleasing for Andrew Ridgeley, for at the turn of the year he had remarked, somewhat tongue in cheek, 'Where's our Number 1?' at a CBS sales conference and was loudly booed in the process! It also earned Wham! their second gold disc for sales over 500,000, 'Wake Me Up Before You Go Go' having supplied their first.

November was an exceptional month for the group, with their second album 'Make It Big' entering the UK charts at Number 1 and 'Wake Me Up Before You Go Go' sliding into the top spot in the US in the same week. The album followed the same path trodden by 'Fantastic'; George wrote all but one of the tracks (including 'Careless Whisper' which as previously mentioned was co-written with Andrew) and produced and arranged the entire album. The one track George didn't have a hand in writing was a cover of the Isley Brothers 'If You Were There'.

'Make It Big' would spend two weeks on top and a total of 72 weeks on the UK chart. Yet it was the American success of the album that had been the real icing on the cake, for prior to its launch George had said **"It frightens me. I know it is going to take up all our time unless we really put a clamp on it and say, we're taking this place – like it or not. America can come slowly. It doesn't have to come in a blast. If it did, it would probably kill us."** The chart-topping run at home came to an end with their next release, with 'Everything She Wants'/'Last Christmas' peaking at Number 2. Its failure to grab the top spot was not a surprise, nor would Wham! lose any credibility, for they were kept out by an altogether more important record. The autumn of 1984 had been dominated by the news of a major famine sweeping across Africa and nightly news bulletins brought the horror of the situation into everyone's homes.

While the assorted aid agencies were doing all they could to alleviate the situation, Bob Geldof (of the Boomtown Rats) and Midge Ure (from Ultravox) decided to do a little bit more. Gathering a few of their friends into Band Aid (in effect a Who's Who of British pop music) they recorded 'Do They Know It's Christmas?' – and George Michael was one of the featured soloists on a record that touched the imagination of the public.

As Bob Geldof would so rightly point out, the simple gesture of buying a record would ultimately mean the difference between living and dying for those in Africa, and over three million copies were sold in the UK – where the single held onto the Number 1 spot for five weeks – and nearly a million copies in the US, where it made the Top 20 and inspired a like-minded effort by USA For Africa entitled 'Feed The World'.

20 **GEORGE MICHAEL** READ WITHOUT PREJUDICE

CHAPTER TWO **MAKING IT BIG** 21

Though it was all for a good cause, George did not entirely enjoy the process of recording 'Do They Know It's Christmas?'. 'I felt very uncomfortable in the studio when we did the Band Aid thing,' he admitted. 'I was very aware of the prejudice against Wham! in there. Everybody in there had said things about everyone else in the press and, to a lot of people, Wham! were the laughing stock of the year. Some of it was jealousy and some of it was a genuine lack of respect.'

Despite its inability to dislodge Band Aid, there's no doubt that 'Everything She Wants'/'Last Christmas' was a fine single, with over a million members of the public agreeing. What was more, in a little-publicised gesture, royalties from this record would later be added to the growing Band Aid account.

Recognition for what Wham! had achieved over the previous two years was duly given at the Grosvenor House Hotel in February 1985. The fourth annual BRIT Awards (set up as a British equivalent to the American Grammy Awards) and voted for by the record industry gave the Best British Group Award to George and Andrew. Five days later, 'Careless Whisper' topped the US charts to commence its three-week stay.

It was the international success of 'Careless Whisper' and 'Make It Big' that elevated Wham! in general and George Michael in particular into the 'superstar' bracket. The album finally hit the top in the US in March 1985 for three weeks, putting it well on its way to selling five million copies. A few days later, George became the youngest ever winner of the Songwriter of the Year award at the London-staged Ivor Novello Awards, and was clearly emotional at the ceremony when the coveted statuette was handed over by childhood hero Elton John. In addition, 'Careless Whisper' was confirmed as the Most Performed Work.

22 **GEORGE MICHAEL** READ WITHOUT PREJUDICE

Soon after, George and Andrew were packing their suitcases for a tour of China. While artists performing behind the Iron Curtain had now become almost commonplace, no western act had ever been invited behind the Bamboo Curtain, and it took lengthy and intense negotiations between the Chinese Government and Simon Napier-Bell before the final go-ahead was given. The highlights of the brief tour were the opportunity to walk along the famous Chinese Wall and a concert given at the 10,000 capacity Workers Gymnasium in Beijing.

George headed for America soon after Wham! returned to appear with Smokey Robinson and Stevie Wonder in a Motown special. This in itself showed how independent George was becoming from Andrew. When Wham! began their assault on the pop charts, it was Andrew who appeared the more worldly-wise, better able to handle the media and conduct interviews and far more comfortable in front of the camera. The job of being a pop star was one that Andrew Ridgeley could handle. George, on the other hand, was more comfortable in the studio.

The success of 'Careless Whisper' showed him to be an exceptional songwriter and vocalist, the latter quality having resulted in the invitation to join Band Aid. And once back in the UK, George would find himself figuring in Bob Geldof's next fundraising plan, the globally-televised Live Aid concert. George was invited to join Elton John on stage at Wembley, singing 'Don't Let The Sun Go Down On Me' while Elton provided piano accompaniment.

Elton and George had grown close friends since September 1984 when they met in the south of France. There was mutual respect for each other's work, and when Elton later asked George to be a backing vocalist on 'Nikita', George was only too happy to oblige. Elton's single would hit Number 3 just before Christmas that year, while George also featured on 'I'm Your Man', a chart-topper for Wham! in November, and two further Top 10 hits, 'Last Christmas' and 'Do They Know It's Christmas?', both of which were re-released for the Christmas market.

the Final GoGo

CHAPTER THREE

Although the decision wouldn't be made public for a further five months, George and Andrew had already decided in November to formally disband Wham! the following year. The plan was to fix up a farewell tour and concert and then make a public announcement about their future plans. In the meantime there were further honours for the group: Favourite Video, Duo or Group at the American Music Awards in January and an Outstanding Contribution Award at the BRIT Awards the following month.

On the face of it, a second solo George Michael single was not a surprise, but the accompanying announcement that Wham! were to dissolve immediately after their June concert at Wembley Stadium made headline news. As far as the group were concerned, now was as good a time as any to part; they were at the peak of their commercial success and had achieved all their original aims. George had developed into one of the finest songwriters of his generation and had grown in stature and confidence with each passing Wham! release; his immediate future seemed secure. For Andrew Ridgeley, the future was not nearly as well defined. There were those within the tabloid media who had questioned his contribution to the group almost since the first chart breakthrough, while those same reporters had delighted in chronicling the occasional lapse in behaviour. While only George and Andrew ultimately know what each contributed to the group, there is much to commend Andrew's role over the previous four years.

As mentioned earlier, Andrew had been the key figure in interviews in the group's earliest days, mainly because he was the one with the confidence to deal with the media, who knew that they all needed a story and usually ensured they got one, who devised the image, frequently correctly (and once or twice not so correctly, as with the decision to thrust shuttlecocks down their shorts and then fire them into the mainly female audience on one of their early tours!). In either case, he took much of the pressure away from the more creative George.

Matters hadn't been helped by Wham!'s manager Simon Napier-Bell placing stories in the press which supposedly hinted at a major row between George and Andrew being behind the decision to split. George was quick to put the record straight. **"Simon keeps reiterating this point about me looking for an excuse to get rid of Andrew,"** *explained George.* **"He keeps rubbishing our relationship. I'm not going to let Simon do that – he's always thrown such a cynical angle on everything he's been involved in. It makes it all look such a sham. If we weren't friends in the first place we wouldn't have stayed together this long. No way could I have done it without Andrew."** George continued by saying he couldn't think of anybody he'd ever met who would have been **"so perfect in allowing something which started out as a very naive, joint ambition, to become what was still a huge double act but was really mine. I have never met anyone who would be strong or generous enough to let that happen. He contributed so much. It was one of those things that just makes you think it was all meant to happen."**

"The luckiest thing that ever happened to me was meeting Andrew, he totally shaped my life. Not just those years but the whole thing – he totally shaped it and I would never begrudge him that credit. People put him down…you don't defend someone at the dinner table by mentioning that they totally shaped your life. But that's the way I feel about him."

CHAPTER 3 **THE FINAL GO GO** 27

The run-in to that final concert progressed in much the same way Wham! had carried on for the last couple of years: 'A Different Corner', George's second solo single topped the charts in the UK for three weeks (and made the US Top 10), while Wham!'s farewell single, a four track EP with 'The Edge Of Heaven' and 'Where Did Our Love Go' being promoted as a double A-side, hit the top for two weeks, including (fittingly enough) the very week the final concert took place. Over 72,000 crammed into Wembley for 'The Final', as it was termed in true football style, and were treated in turn to an exceptional performance from the group. It might have been their final performance, but they ensured the audience would remember it for a long time to come.

The disbanding of the group was as good a time as any for a retrospective of their career and one month after the concert a compilation release, also entitled 'The Final', hit the shops. Containing all of their hits it proved another instant success, although with Madonna fever sweeping the country at the time it was unable to dislodge her 'True Blue' from the chart summit.

It is also worth mentioning that, while much of the attention at the time Wham! announced their decision to dissolve concerned what would happen to George and Andrew, the two backing singers Shirlie and Pepsi also needed to contemplate their future. In the event, they teamed up in the imaginatively titled Shirlie & Pepsi and would also hit the charts with releases like 'Heartache' (Number 2, January 1987) and 'Goodbye Stranger' (Number 9 in May).

"The final appearance of Wham! at Wembley was incredible, but strangely it was so important to me that it didn't register immediately," George later admitted. **"I don't think I enjoyed it enough, but watching the video now is absolutely stunning. I have never seen a crowd like that – for anyone at any concert, apart perhaps for Live Aid."**

"In retrospect," he concluded, *"I know that it was really perfect. The weather was perfect, the people were perfect and the band was great. Everything in the whole series of Wham! events seemed to be blessed that it was just the cherry on the cake."*

"At the end of Wham! I needed a new challenge. So I set myself the challenge of getting up there on the American level with Madonna and Michael Jackson – that circle of people. That was my goal." George admitted he'd woken up one morning and realised that there had been a period in Wham! when he'd had actually completely forgotten who he was – a lack of self-identity which led to an eight-month depression. 'It was a very self-pitying thing, sense of isolation and all that stuff. I started losing my temper for the first time. I got into fist fights with friends, threw photographers against walls, acted very macho…terrible. In that period I lost my temper six or eight times. I wasn't drunk so there was no excuse for my behaviour, the people that knew me and who saw me like this were horrified. I'd go completely out of character.

"My voice would drop about an octave and I'd start talking with this incredibly heavy slang. A lot of it was not having a person there to say to me, 'Look, what have you got to complain about?' A combination of things set it off. Wham! split up and I came out of a bad relationship. For a time I thought I really didn't want to get back into the music business when we finished Wham! The problem was just that I had developed a character for the outside world that wasn't me, and I was having to deal with people all the time who thought it was.' George concluded he needed a period to put things into perspective – and the answer was a consultation with 'Doctor' Ridgeley. *"I went out to see Andrew in LA and got pissed out of my head and poured it all out,"* he reveals. *"Until that moment, the way I felt and what I was really thinking hadn't crystallised. When I heard it actually come out of my own mouth it was like an exorcism."*

30 **GEORGE MICHAEL** READ WITHOUT PREJUDICE

CHAPTER 3 **THE FINAL GO GO** 31

Different Corners

CHAPTER FOUR

By the time George had got the depression out of the way, sessions were booked for SARM Studios in London and PUK Studios in Denmark and he was busy writing material for what would eventually form the 'Faith' album. Then, in September, he flew to America to record 'I Knew You Were Waiting (For Me)', a song written by Simon Climie and Dennis Morgan which was to be a duet with soul legend Aretha Franklin. The session was produced by Narada Michael Walden, himself a noteworthy recording artist but who became internationally renowned when he concentrated on production. The resulting single, released on Epic in the UK and Arista (Aretha's label) in the US eventually topped the charts on both sides of the Atlantic in 1987.

There was one final event that required George's attention before the year was out; his own solo contract with Epic. When the label had picked up Wham!'s contract from Innervision it had made sure that both George and Andrew were signed as separate entities as well as members of the group, and so when Wham! formally announced their intention of going their own separate ways, Epic picked up the options for both artists.

For George, this meant he was contracted to provide Epic with at least five albums. Andrew was able to go into semi-retirement from the music industry, turning instead to motor racing and acting with little success before resuming his musical career with the self-penned 'Son Of Albert' album and 'Shake' single in 1990. This, too, was only moderately successful, although Andrew handled the resulting media interest extremely well. Once his brief moment of solo fame was over, he slipped back into retirement, moving down to the west country.

George released his first solo single as a solo artist in June 1987 and it showed a remarkable departure from the kind of material he had been writing for Wham! 'I Want Your Sex' was considerably funkier than anything he had previously recorded, as one might have expected. After all, Wham! had become major heroes of the teen market; George was going to aim his material at an older, more sophisticated market, preferably without alienating his existing fans if at all possible.

To begin with it wasn't his fans among the record buying public he had to worry about, but those within the media. For a while they had fully supported each and every Wham! release since the group first made their chart breakthrough, but 'I Want Your Sex' was to prove a different matter. It wasn't the quality, it was the content. Although the single would ultimately benefit from its inclusion on the soundtrack to the smash hit film *Beverly Hills Cop II* (starring Eddie Murphy), the single was not universally accepted; Radio 1 would only play the record after 9.00pm (a supposed watershed when children would be in bed) and MTV demanded three recuts before airing the video.

George could hardly believe the controversy the record caused. **"American rap music and heavy metal are so aggressively sexual in a completely distasteful way – and I didn't think 'I Want Your Sex' was at all,"** he argued. **"I like the idea of it being aggressively sexual, but you had to get the idea that the aggression was the lust. The only way I was going to get the sex was with consent. It wasn't about trying to make someone do something – it was trying to show how much you wanted them."** George claimed he wasn't at all comfortable with being a sex spokesman. **"I didn't see why anyone should ask me. I wanted to reach a new bunch of fans with the single, and it worked well in the States. But I couldn't attract new fans in Britain – because of the IBA ban, nobody heard it."**

Despite, or perhaps even because of the controversy, the record still made Number 3 in the UK and Number 2 in the US. There was further controversy the following month for George to contend with, although this time he retained a diplomatic silence. The cause this time was a cover version of the Bee Gees' 'Jive Talkin'', credited to Boogie Box High. It was claimed that the actual artist was George's cousin and that George was at least a backing vocalist on the single that hit the Top 10 in the UK. But since no-one admitted who was on the record, that was one mystery that still awaits solving.

CHAPTER FOUR **DIFFERENT CORNERS** 35

It was back on safer ground for the next single, the title track to his forthcoming 'Faith' album. As different a sound as any he had tried previously, the Buddy Holly soundalike 'Faith' was an instant smash at radio and with the public, hitting Number 2 in the UK and Number 1 for four weeks in the US. The single, however, was merely a taster for the album. According to George, the songs on the album **"...are the results of two years of my life. They are dedicated to my family and friends, whose loyalty and time are more important to me than ever before."** George wrote all of the songs on the album (although 'Look At Your Hands' was co-written with David Austin), as well as producing and arranging all of the material. He also played most of the instruments – this was very much a solo album

"To me the album was about the affirmation of faith – because before that period of my life there had been a lack of it," he explained. "Coming out of the Wham! thing I felt as if some big joke had been played on me. I led myself to believe I had everything – I dreamed of realising certain aspirations and they had all happened but I still felt there was a big gap, a massive hole in my life that I was never going to be able to fill. That was the way I felt at the end of Wham! What 'Faith' meant – the album, the campaign, all of it – was that I had faith life was going to deliver, that I was going to get the things I wanted, that my life would bring me the things that are important to me.' The new sound was deemed highly acceptable by the public; the album crashed into the UK album charts in pole position and would ultimately top the US charts for 12 weeks on its way to selling over nine million copies. The British record industry also appreciated what George was achieving, naming him Best British Male Artist at the BRIT Awards the following February. His record company appreciated his worth; they once again renegotiated his contract. And tickets for his forthcoming world tour were as eagerly snapped up in Tokyo as they were in Texas; George Michael had swiftly arrived as one of the major stars of the music world.

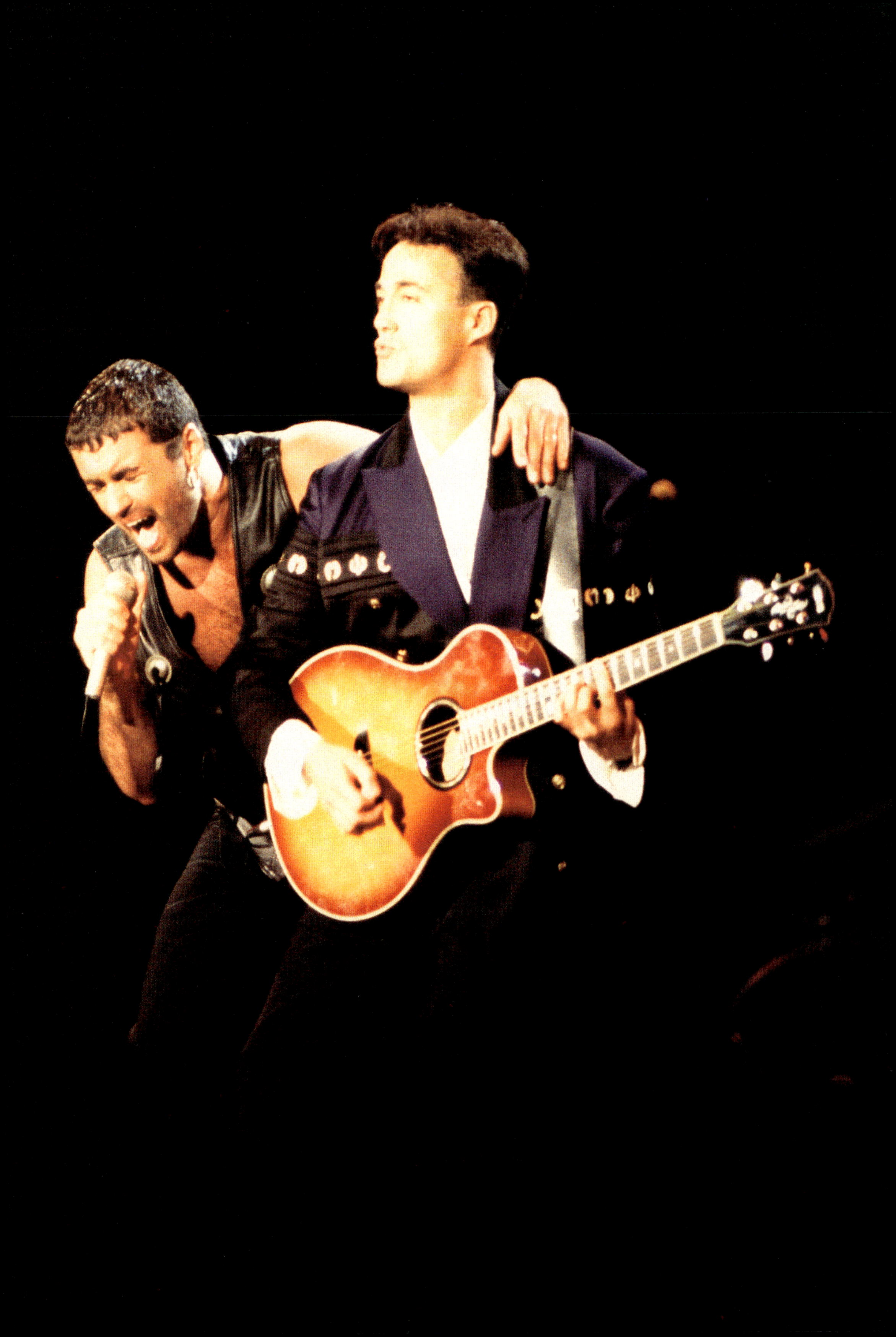

38 **GEORGE MICHAEL** READ WITHOUT PREJUDICE

CHAPTER FOUR **DIFFERENT CORNERS**

Yet stiffer competition than ever on the UK singles chart meant that not all of his singles could or would hit Number 1; 'Father Figure' stalled at Number 11, 'One More Try' at Number 8 and 'Monkey' Number 13 (despite a remix by noted US producers Jimmy Jam and Terry Lewis), but in the UK each successive single ensured further exposure for the album, and 'Faith' remained on the chart for 72 weeks.

It was the US that was to prove most successful for a solo George Michael. In the 12 months between February 1988 and February 1989, George hit the top spot on the US singles chart with all three releases. Add 'Faith' to the list and the final tally of four chart-toppers from a single parent album was an exceptional feat. It gave George a total of eight US Number 1s during the decade, a figure only bettered by Michael Jackson.

And the US awards kept piling up; a Grammy for Best R&B Performance By A Duo Or Group With Vocal for 'I Knew You Were Waiting (For Me)' with Aretha Franklin, Best Direction award at the MTV Video Music Awards, and, perhaps the most prestigious award of all, the Album Of The Year at the 1989 Grammy Awards. The album was effectively a one-man industry, for even a collection of the videos (also including another hit single off the album, 'Kissing A Fool') was a further instant best-seller.

George Michael could do no wrong in 1988. His appearance at the Nelson Mandela 70th Birthday Tribute at Wembley had been eagerly awaited, and if there was some disappointment when his entire performance consisted of cover versions of other artists' material, then few made their unhappiness known. At the end of the year, his contract with his record company was once again amended.

FREEdom

CHAPTER FIVE

After such success, it was not surprising when George was named Songwriter of the Year (for the second time) at the Ivor Novello Awards in April 1989. In fact, the whole year seemed devoted to travelling the globe and collecting awards of one kind or another, as well as beginning work on 'Listen Without Prejudice', the follow-up album. Recorded at SARM West and Metropolis Studios in London, 'Listen Without Prejudice Volume 1' was already shaping up to be one of the most eagerly awaited albums of the 1990s. When excited CBS executives heard the tapes for the first time in July 1990, they renegotiated George's contract once again!

Little wonder, then, that the *Sunday Times* had listed George in their annual list of the 200 richest people, placing him at 128 with a fortune estimated at £65 million. Whether the figure is or was correct wasn't the issue, the fact that a paper as prestigious as the *Sunday Times* estimated him to be that rich was indication enough of the potential earning power of the top musicians in the country.

The album was officially to be released in September, but the month before George appeared on BBC Radio 1's *Steve Wright Show* to talk about the album and potential singles. Even so, he gave no indication of the potential bombshell that was about to hit the musical world.

The album was previewed in early September by the release of 'Praying For Time' as a single. As before, it proved to be a bigger success on the American charts, hitting Number 1 in October after stalling at Number 6 in the UK. George received more than adequate compensation when the album was released; it was an instant Number 1 in the UK. At the same time, George released his autobiography *Bare* (co-written with Tony Parsons) and announced to a shocked media that he intended turning his back on the traditional trappings of being a pop star; he no longer wished to appear in his own videos, would not be conducting interviews or touring. Instead, he wanted to concentrate on songwriting.

The autobiography was especially revealing: **"When I decided to split with Andrew I was in the middle of a very heavy depression, drinking too much and taking drugs. I had personal problems at the time. I was going through the end of a relationship and I was feeling very negative about the whole Wham! thing. I was feeling trapped by a lot of things. I can honestly say I never lost my temper until I was in my twenties. And then for a period of about six or eight months before the end of Wham! I really lost it."** The move, almost without precedent, was hard to understand. There were elements the media (or at least the public) could appreciate, not least the desire for a bit more privacy. But artists such as Prince and Michael Jackson, while hardly known for their eloquence at interviews, did at least deign to appear in their own videos. How could a record company promote an artist who appeared to have no wish to be promoted? Time would tell if it was a wise move on George's part.

In January 1991, George was scheduled to make an appearance at the Rock In Rio II festival at the world famous Maracana Stadium in Rio de Janeiro, performing on the 25th and then closing the festival three days later. On that closing show, the band struck up the familiar opening bars to 'Careless Whisper', with George introducing the song with 'Now I'd like to bring on a great friend of mine, Andrew Ridgeley, who wrote this song ten years ago.' With that Andrew strode out on stage to be greeted by a deafening roar of approval from the 100,000 crowd. The reunion went down a storm, the crowd appreciating every number the pair performed.

Afterwards, George said **"It was something we wanted to do just once, to show people we were proud of what we did. It was an incredibly night. I've never known an atmosphere like it. It was very emotional when Andrew came on. We are still the greatest of friends."**

CHAPTER FIVE **FREEDOM** 43

44 **GEORGE MICHAEL** READ WITHOUT PREJUDICE

CHAPTER FIVE **FREEDOM** 45

Andrew agreed. *"It was a very special night – we had a great time. After a few bars of 'I'm Your Man' I looked over at George and it was like nothing had changed. We were two mates enjoying ourselves again."*

Meanwhile, it appeared to be business as usual as 'Listen…' began its seemingly relentless march up the American charts. It was only when it stalled at Number 2, held off the top by MC Hammer's 'Please Hammer Don't Hurt 'Em' that chinks began to appear in the armour. A second single, 'Waiting For That Day', could only get as high as Number 23 in the UK. A third release, 'Freedom 90' (the 90 was added to differentiate it from the earlier Wham! release) fared worse, stalling at Number 28 in the UK and Number 8 in the US. Even the accompanying video seemed to confirm George's intentions; crammed with 'supermodels' and containing one scene in which his familiar leather jacket was burnt.

George appeared to relent in early 1991 when he announced plans for a concert tour of the UK, but audiences up and down the country were mystified at the choice of material. While most of the songs he performed were well known, they weren't his! If the audience had wanted to hear 'Killer', they would probably have bought tickets to either Adamski or Seal dates. Where were the numbers George was known for, such as 'Faith', 'Father Figure' or 'One More Try'? One report noted even a show containing all of Wham!'s hits would have been preferable!

If topping 'Faith' was proving to be a difficult task (and it was always likely to be, with or without George's support), then 'Listen Without Prejudice' was not without its own moments of glory, culminating in George receiving the Best British Album award at the 1991 BRIT Awards. Speaking of the album, George said

"I've never made an album that sounds like 'Listen Without Prejudice' before. When I came up with the title for the album, I was warned by a lot of people that it looked like I was saying don't be prejudiced against me. But what I was talking about was that the album should be listened to by all types and races."

George believed that radio and video over the last three or four years had gone into two directions – one for white people and one for black. ***"In the mid 1980s,"** he continued, **"black and white crossover music was a real hip thing to do, but now it seems quite the opposite. You're supposed to know who you're aiming your music at and who you should be listening to, depending on your colour."*** If dealing with diminishing record sales wasn't enough problems to be going on with for George, there then came a monumental move on behalf of CBS – the company was sold to the Japanese electronics giant Sony. The move was a bombshell on many fronts, not least that CBS was one of the truly great American record companies indeed, one of the truly great American companies period. Aside from the record industry, the company had interests in radio, television and book publishing. In short, just about every possible aspect of the communications industry.

The recording arm had enjoyed unparalleled success during the 1980s, not least thanks to Michael Jackson's 'Thriller' (48 million copies sold worldwide), 'Faith' (14 million), Bruce Springsteen's 'Born In The USA' (12 million sales in the US alone) and a host of other multi-million sellers. Artists of the calibre of Bob Dylan, Barbra Streisand, Julio Iglesias, Santana, Luther Vandross and the Rolling Stones were on the company's books at some time during the decade. CBS was the world's biggest and most successful record company. It was a surprise when it was announced that the company was to be sold, even more surprising that it should be sold to the Japanese.

However, at the beginning of the 1980s, Sony's Betamax video format lost out in a battle with VHS, mainly because more of the films that people wanted to watch were available on that format. Sony reasoned that such a situation would not happen with any future technological developments, such as MiniDisc; so they paid $2 billion to acquire CBS Records.

Electronic companies buying heavily into the record industry was not new – Phillips own Phonogram, Polydor, A&M and Island, while Thorn-EMI have bought Virgin and Chrysalis – but the scale of the deal was still surprising.

There were and still are numerous artists' contracts that contained 'key man clauses'; in the event that the artist and repertoire manager or chief executive of the record company you were signed to happened to be poached and go off to join another company, your contract became null and void and you would be able to move with him. It is unlikely there were any clauses in any of CBS and Epic's artists contract covering the possible sale of the company since no-one expected it to happen!

But it did – and more than one or two artists appeared less than happy at the dramatic news and the perceived change in direction the company was taking. The most vociferous of these was George Michael. Already aggrieved at the performance of 'Listen', he stopped touring altogether. Then he announced he wouldn't be making any more records for CBS/Sony and that he wanted out of his contract. This obviously wasn't going to be an easy matter!

It has been claimed that a second volume of 'Listen…' was already in the can at the time George handed over the tapes to the first volume. True or not, the second album didn't materialise. Perhaps George hoped that by withholding the albums he was contracted to deliver, CBS would sue him for breach of contract. The easiest solution then for all concerned would be for the record company to release him from his contract, leaving him free to go and sign – and sing – for someone else.

The record company didn't see it that way; if he wasn't going to sing for them then he wouldn't be able to sing for anyone else either, at least until his contract ran out. All of this was at this point conjecture, because no writs would be issued until much later.

Against this backdrop of growing legal problems, it's remarkable how much George Michael's material did find its way to the public, albeit in the form of duets, But the success of these ensured George was seldom out of the news for one reason or another over the next four to five years!

Long-term friend and confidante Elton John had joined George on stage during one tour and the pair had sung the song that had been so well received at Live Aid in 1985, 'Don't Let The Sun Go Down On Me' which was recorded live and duly released in the UK in December 1991. It crashed into the chart at Number 1 and spent two weeks in the pole position, subsequently repeating the feat in the US. Proceeds from the single in the UK were handed over to the London Lighthouse (AIDS) and Rainbow Trust charities, while in the US the Dana Farber Cancer Institute was the charity to benefit.

CHAPTER FIVE **FREEDOM** 49

Healing the PAIN

CHAPTER SIX

When George Michael launched his legal battle to get himself out of the contract he had signed with Epic/CBS, one of his main bones of contention was the reduced sales figure for 'Listen Without Prejudice' as opposed to 'Faith', especially in the US. This was certainly true, but no one suggested that Michael Jackson should similarly sue when 'Bad' failed to match 'Thriller', or Bruce Springsteen's 'Tunnel Of Love' fell short of 'Born In The USA'. And the relevance of selecting either of these acts is that they both recorded for CBS or its offshoots. It has also to be said in defence of the record company that they would undoubtedly have done all they could with the materials at their disposal; George's decision to reject much of the traditional lifestyle associated with rock stars, like making videos and conducting interviews ultimately hurt him far more than it did them. True, making videos and telling the same story to different journalists around the world, the endless travelling, the unwarranted intrusions into your privacy and the numerous business meetings are part of the down side associated with the rock industry (and it undoubtedly *is* an industry). But they are more than compensated for by the level of earnings today's top performers (of which George Michael is a member of the élite clan) can command. And while only those closely involved in the drawing up and signing of the numerous contracts will be fully aware of the financial implications, the record company agreed to renegotiate on numerous occasions, all of which were duly signed by the artist.

It has also to be said that George's main argument appeared to be with the American record company and its new Japanese owners, not the UK company that had shown so much faith in him (and Andrew and the other members of Wham!) back in 1982. Indeed, George dedicated his Best British Album award at the 1991 BRIT Awards to Ronnie Fischer, the Epic product manager who had died the previous November.

In October 1991, George attended a meeting with Sony's world president Norio Ohga, Sony Music UK head Paul Russell, Michael Schulhof, head of Sony Music worldwide, manager Rob Kahane and publisher Dick Leahy. George quickly outlined his grievances – the record company had changed beyond all recognition to the one he had originally signed with. Furthermore, on the basis that there had been little promotion for 'Listen Without Prejudice' in the US, he had lost faith in them, perhaps in the same way they had lost faith in him over his refusal to tour or make videos.

Under such circumstances, it would be in everyone's interest if he was allowed to leave the label and sign for someone else. And rather than resort to the courts, the settlement should be reached by those present at the meeting. He left convinced they would see things his way – they didn't, for the next day he was told there would not be a 'quickie' divorce.

That decision meant that George would have to take the matter to court if he wished to leave the label. His lawyer Tony Russell fired the first broadside a couple of days after Sony had made their position known; Epic lacked both the creative and marketing abilities to handle George Michael's product, that George would not be bound by his contract and owned the master tapes. While Tony Russell put the High Court writ together, there were already strong indications that the case would not reach the courts before October 1993 – and that meant there would still be no new George Michael material for the foreseeable future.

The writ was duly served on 30 October, claiming the contract George signed in January 1988 was so heavily weighted in favour of Sony Music that it amounted to restraint of trade. The writ also claimed that Sony owned all of George's recordings, even though recording costs had been deducted from royalties and therefore paid by George. And such were the terms of the contract George had with Sony, for every copy of 'Faith' and 'Listen Without Prejudice' sold, George received 57p while Sony earned £1.83. That was for vinyl versions of the album; for CDs Sony made £3.38 while George got 69p.

The writ also pointed out that nine per cent of George's album sales did not pay any royalties because of the high number of 'free' units given to wholesalers and retailers. George, it claimed had no power of audit over Sony outside the UK, that Sony could dictate what was released and when, and that George could not appear in any film produced by a third party.

CHAPTER SIX **HEALING THE PAIN** 53

While Tony Russell was serving the writ, George Michael was making his own announcement. **"Since Sony Corporation bought my contract, along with everything and everyone else at CBS, I have seen the great American company that I proudly signed to as a teenager become a small part of the production line for a giant electronics corporation which, quite frankly, has no understanding of the creative process. Sony appears to see artists as little more than software. Musicians do not come in regimented shapes and sizes but are individuals who evolve together. Sony views this as a great inconvenience."** Sony's comment was brief and to the point. **"Our contract with George is valid and legally binding. There is a serious moral as well as legal commitment to any contract, and we will not only honour it but vigorously defend it."**

While the two sets of lawyers began putting their respective cases together, there was one further record featuring George Michael that hit the shops during the summer of 1992. George had appeared at the Freddie Mercury tribute concert held at Wembley in April – six months after the death of the flamboyant Queen frontman – and four tracks, 'Somebody To Love' (with the remaining members of Queen), 'These Are The Days Of Our Lives' (with Lisa Stansfield), 'Papa Was A Rolling Stone'/'Killer' and 'Calling You', were issued on the Hollywood label. This EP also debuted on the charts at Number 1, although it was classified as an album for the US market and only peaked at Number 46.

The George Michael versus Sony Music case finally came to court in London on 4 October 1993, with George's QC Mark Cran making his opening comments. It promised to be an interesting case to say the least; the public and press galleries were packed, with many expecting to get a brief insight into the pop industry.

According to Mr Cran, the relationship between the record company and artist started to turn sour when he decided to change his image. **"He wanted to play down his image as a sex symbol and play up the quality of his music. To that end he entitled his next album 'Listen Without Prejudice'. He was determined not to associate his image with the record. No pictures of him appeared on the sleeve. But unfortunately he feels that CBS American Division did not support him which led to considerable unhappiness. In the UK, after a slight disagreement, Sony put their backing behind it and it outsold 'Faith'."**

George took the stand on 28 October to be grilled by Sony's counsel QC Gordon Pollock. Under questioning George agreed that he had effectively blackmailed his first record company (Innervision) into renegotiating Wham!'s contract by refusing to hand over the tapes to their debut album.

Of his decision to change his image after the 'Faith' album he said **"As long as the quality of music was maintained they (his female audience in particular) would have moved along with me. I believe that, regardless of my public position or possible financial ramifications for Sony, I have the right to change as a person and artist. I had hoped that, having been a great asset for almost a decade, I would be supported in these changes. Sony have by and large refused that support."**

CHAPTER SIX **HEALING THE PAIN** 57

The exchanges between Gordon Pollock and George Michael were often heated. George refused to state publicly what he was worth, although he did concede he was extraordinarily wealthy and insisted on writing down the sum he believed he was worth and passing it to the judge. **"That is supposed to be a decimal point?"** quipped Mr Pollock when shown the figure. The contents of what George wrote down have been the subject of considerable speculation, with estimates of his fortune ranging from a low of £35 million to a high of £80 million.

What he had or had not earned was not the issue, according to his counsel. What was at stake was the disproportion between what Sony earned from George; on sales of £99.5 million, Sony had received £52.45 million profit, while George had to make do with £7.35 million after recording costs were subtracted.

The hearing lasted for 74 days, finally finishing on 13 April. There would then be a tense two-month wait while Justice Jonathan Parker considered his verdict. That was duly delivered on 21 June.

George was in court, together with his parents Jack and Lesley Panos, to hear the lengthy verdict, which ultimately found in favour of Sony. George could only shake his head as the judgement was read out as the evidence presented by George's American manager Rob Kahane (he stepped down as manager in November of that year) was slammed, with the judge describing him as **"a thoroughly unreliable and untrustworthy witness, whose evidence was coloured by an intense dislike of Sony. Had Sony seen more of Mr Michael and less of Mr Kahane from 1990 onwards, events might have turned out differently."**

In the judge's opinion, the case brought by George Michael failed on four points; that the contract had been renegotiated, that Sony had accepted and paid a request for a million dollars advance, Sony's additional agreement to pay the £11 million and George's constant access to legal advice showed that the company had been extremely fair in their dealings with the artist.

The singer recovered his composure for a press conference later that day. **"I'm shocked at the judgement,"** he confessed. **"It means that even though I both created and paid for my work, I will never own it or have any rights over it. And perhaps most importantly, I have no right to resign. In fact, there is no such thing as resignation of an artist in the music industry. However, I'm convinced that the English legal system will not uphold what is effectively professional slavery."** By the time he got home that evening the enormity of the ruling had hit him. Telephone callers to his Hampstead home were created with the familiar tune to 'Careless Whisper', but with new lyrics: **"I'm never gonna to sing again. Bastards! Bastards!"** The entire record industry had been watching the case with interest, for the contracts of just about every major artist would have been virtually declared void had George won his case. There were many who were critical of the stand he had taken and who took delight in watching him lose his case. But as far as George Michael was concerned, this wasn't the end of the matter or the battle. As he saw it he had two options; he would be appealing against the decision, right the way up to the European Court of Human Rights if necessary in order to get the decision reversed.

If he was still unsuccessful, then he would simply not make another record until his contract with Sony expired in 2003. He was already determined that he had recorded his last ever song for the company, and therefore it would be in everyone's best interests if he was allowed to leave. The news got worse for George; he would have to pay both sides' costs, estimated so far at a cool £3 million.

CHAPTER SIX **HEALING THE PAIN** 59

A few days after the hearing ended, George was interviewed on television by Sir David Frost and set out virtually the entire history of his dealings with CBS and Sony. **"It wasn't a perfect deal because all of the way through I never signed a new deal. Signing a piece of paper which updates the deal, I mean, every single deal that I have done, every single re-negotiation that I've ever done, whether it be with CBS or Sony, has been an extension of the deal that I signed when I was 18 years old, which effectively bound me for, I think it was ten albums actually altogether. It was five and an optional five which is effectively the whole of my career, I imagine. I've never been able to sign a piece of paper as a new deal. I've always been trying to update that deal that I did when I was 18, so I've always been held to that part of the deal that I signed when I was 18 years old."**

"People threw around the figures, these massive figures and massive amounts of money that I was supposedly given by Sony. Now, I will completely agree that they are massive amounts of money, and I am fully aware that I am in a business which pays amazing money, but CBS signed Wham! in 1983. Everything I have been given by Sony, whether it was in 1984, whether it was in 1988, 1990 they have never been giving me anything above the royalties that I had already earned."

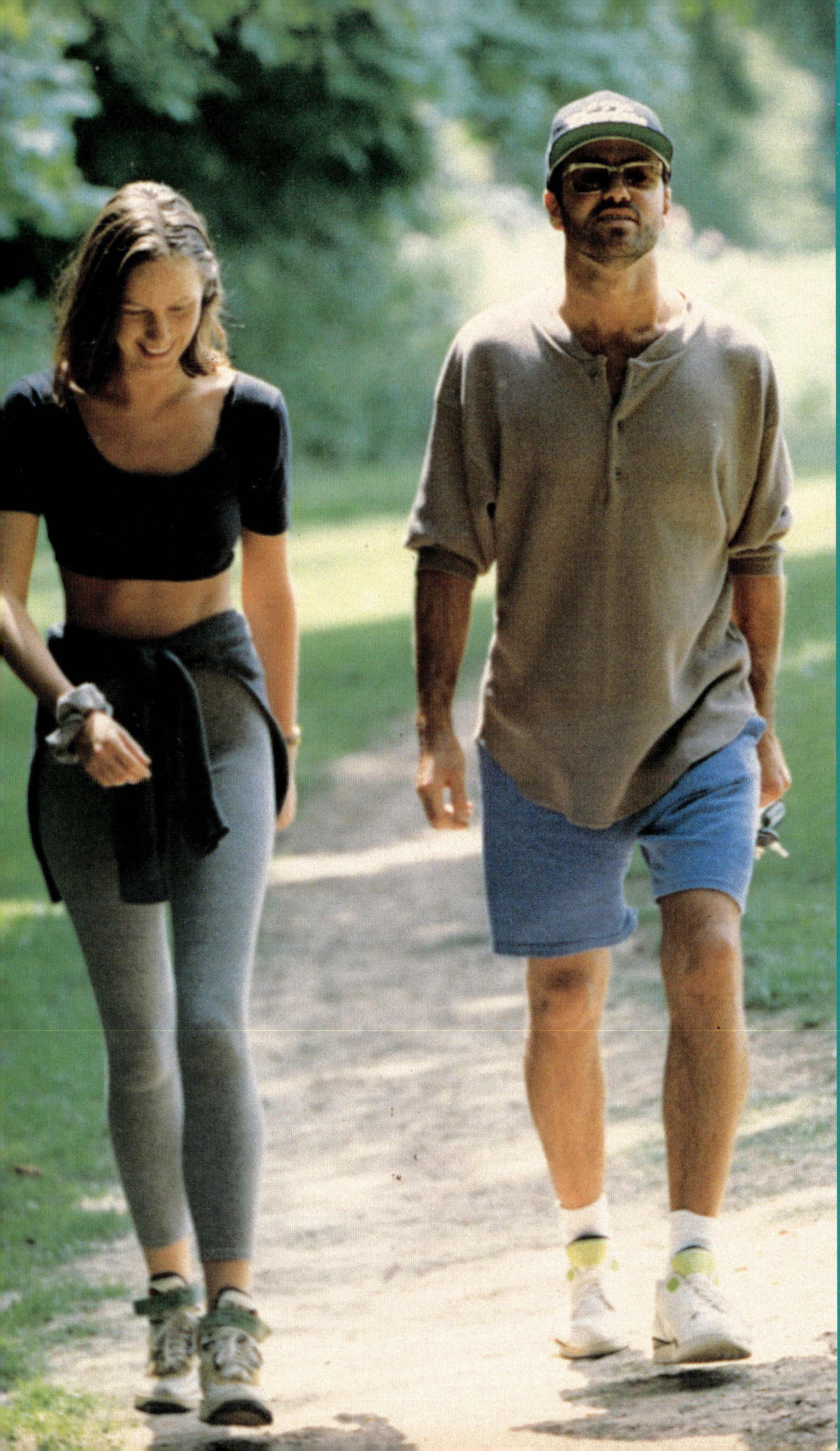

CHAPTER SIX **HEALING THE PAIN** 61

"I was paid £11 million. Actually, I didn't realise that I had been paid £11 million, that came out in the court case but I was paid a huge amount of money – and I know it's a vast amount of money – in 1988, but I was never given anything that CBS or then, Sony, had already collected from the public. They were always in profit with me. No one ever did me a favour, and said, 'Here George, here's £11 million, you know, let's see if we can make it back.' They were always working in the black, as it were." George claimed record companies as a whole were almost always signing people in a very vulnerable position, and that had included him at the age of 18. *"Whenever they're signed, they're desperate. There isn't one other industry that operates on this basis. If I were an author, and I fell out with my company in the way that I have, the worst that I would have to endure was the fact that they would have the first option on my next book, so you're talking about two books. It's a ridiculous situation to sign a contract when you're 18 years old, and to be held to it for your entire professional career. Why, why, would any court uphold that situation?"*

The judge had found, he believed, that he'd reaffirmed his contract at the given point of my re-negotiations – but did he have any choice? The choice, George said, was to go along with that length of term, or to do what he had done now. He wasn't, he claimed, looking for public sympathy. *'I just don't believe that if you are wealthy…that you are not supposed to fight for your principles."*

62 **GEORGE MICHAEL** READ WITHOUT PREJUDICE

CHAPTER SIX **HEALING THE PAIN** 63

"The trouble is that this business is not like working in an office, or working for a company. If you really fall out with people who control your professional life, you have a right to walk away. Most people, in whatever situation in life, in whatever job, have the right to say... 'If you don't want me anymore, if you don't want to work with me anymore, if you don't like the way I work, well, sod you! I'm going elsewhere. I may take a smaller wage packet. I may have to work somewhere I don't like as much as this building. I may have to do all kinds of things I don't want to, but I'm free to do it.' That is the right of every individual, and the music industry takes away that right from every artist it signs." George revealed that it had got to the stage that for the first time in his career, Sony in the US was refusing to release the singles he wanted in the succession he wanted, *"and I have always had a very clear idea of which order singles should be released"*. Eventually, once the album was effectively dead in the US, even though it was still selling around the world, they had just said they didn't want to release any more singles. To George, that represented deliberately not exploiting his material. *"The judgement itself, I thought, was bizarre. I thought it was a very strange judgement. The judge was kind enough to point out that he believed I was very honest and candid in the witness box, so I did my best to be truthful and at the same time, he completely accepted everybody on Sony's side. Everybody that appeared in defence of Sony...he completely accepted that they were all telling the truth. Now, if they were all telling the truth about the events that happened between 1990, and the time the writ was served, then, why was I not lying? Somebody was lying."*

"The ultimate truth is Sony didn't need me to begin with. Sony as a corporation is so massive, and even as a record company it is so massive that they can do without George Michael perfectly easily. The UK company would miss me, the company as a whole would not miss me because it has so many major artists. What they did mean to do with this court case was hold on to their standard contract, and with this judgement they've managed to do that."

"If they (Sony) were that responsible, this would never have got to court in the first place. If they had been reasonable I could have said look, I don't want to tell the world that this is going on, please let me go. I've been with you for ten years, I've made you hundreds of millions of dollars, and people will believe the deal is over, you know, I've been here this long. They wouldn't accept that. They wouldn't come close to accepting that. I have no real reason to believe that they'll be reasonable before the court of appeal, so, I think, that ultimately, I think it's going to end up in the court of appeal. It's not what I want, but, I think, that's where it's going to end up."

George was trying not to look beyond the possibility of the appeal, but left the door open for Sony to approach him.

"If they were to come to me at this stage and say, 'OK, George, we've made our point, you can go, we really don't need you...you can continue your career elsewhere, you know we don't want this mess to continue,' I have to be honest. If they were going to do that unconditionally, I'd have to say, 'OK, I'm not going to be a martyr, I have my own life to think about, and I can't fight for the whole industry at the risk of losing the rest – or the next ten years – of my life as an artist.' And I would probably accept that."

CHAPTER SIX **HEALING THE PAIN** 65

George duly lodged his appeal on 8 August amid mounting speculation that it would never come to court and that wheels were being turned behind the scenes to come up with a solution. The proposed plan was for George to be transferred to another label, just as though he was a footballer. Given the importance of the artist and the sum Sony would be looking to receive, it meant that only a handful of labels had a realistic chance of signing him, but at least almost everyone would get some degree of satisfaction from the deal.

The following month the American recording industry association RIAA certified 'Listen Without Prejudice' double platinum, thereby seeming to contradict George's criticism of the American record company. By the year's end, 'Faith' would be certified a nine million seller Stateside.

While George waited to hear when his appeal would be heard, he finally performed a new song at the inaugural MTV European Music Awards. The new single, 'Jesus To A Child', was considerably more mellow than previous George Michael efforts but extremely well received all the same. The only speculation concerned what label would get to release the new single, for three weeks later Sir Thomas Bingham, the Court of Appeal's Master of the Rolls, informed the star that his appeal was unlikely to be heard before 1996.

MovingON

CHAPTER SEVEN

Early 1995 was filled with considerable rumour – not least that it looked likely that George would win his freedom from his Sony contract and that two labels, Virgin in the UK and the new Dreamworks SKG in America, would be the ultimate winners. All this assumed that Sony would give way to George's demands. In April, 'Jesus To A Child' got another airing, this time exclusively on Capital Radio. The playing of the record raised considerable funds for their 'Help A London Child' charity. And still the outcome of the court case remained in the balance.

The matter was finally resolved in July, with an announcement that Sony were prepared to release George from his contract and that the singer would be signing a two-album deal with Dreamworks SKG for the US and Virgin Records for the rest of the world. The new deal supposedly guaranteed Sony some $40 million, three per cent of the retail value of those two albums, plus the rights to his back catalogue and to put together a greatest hits package.

It was an expensive deal by almost any stretch of the imagination – but then again the record industry had become used to such sums, thanks largely to the highly publicised deals two members of the Jackson clan, Michael and Janet, had concluded with their respective companies (interestingly enough, Sony and Virgin!). More importantly for George, he had secured his freedom from Sony. Fascinatingly, though, his next action was to appoint Andy Stephens, vice-president of Sony Music Europe, as his new manager for the world outside North America!

The music world waited with bated breath for the new George Michael single, his first since his troubles with Sony first emerged. The stately ballad 'Jesus To A Child' was serviced to the waiting radio stations digitally via satellite on 12 December and the following month entered the UK charts at Number 1, displacing Michael Jackson's 'Earth Song' after a six-week residency at the chart summit. Although 'Jesus To A Child' only remained at Number 1 for one week, it was ample proof that the enforced absence from the music industry had done little to dent George Michael's popularity. When the following month the single hit the American Top 10 (it peaked at Number 7), it seemed almost as though he hadn't been away.

In fairness, the publicity George Michael had both enjoyed and endured during the previous four years had made it relatively simple to ensure a high chart placing. Final proof would come with the all-important second single from his even more important album. In May, the highly danceable and frankly hedonistic 'Fastlove' – quoting musically from Patrice Rushen's 'Forget Me Nots' – repeated the performance of its predecessor and entered the chart at Number 1, this time remaining in pole position for three weeks.

If the single had held on for just one more week, then George would have held prime positions on both the singles and album charts, for 'Older', his first album in some six years, similarly entered the chart at Number 1. In the United States, 'Fastlove' also made the Top 10, peaking at Number 8, while the album debuted at Number 6. A third UK single, the AIDS-aware love song 'Spinning The Wheel', entered the chart at its Number 2 peak behind the Spice Girls' debut 'Wannabe'.

Another George Michael composition would also find its path to the top blocked by 'Wannabe' – a remake of 'Freedom 90' by ex-Take That singer Robbie Williams, who'd recently celebrated his eventual divorce from the Manchester 'boy band'. He'd claimed to have drawn inspiration from George's fight to control his own destiny – though whether he'd prove as long-lasting a talent very much remained to be seen.

As with 'Faith', promoting George's 'Older' would be seen as a long-term project. There is little doubt that George had remained active as far as his songwriting is concerned while the legal wrangles with Sony were unfolding. Although he may not have been able to release any new material, his life still contained the experiences that have always been central to his songwriting – falling in and out of love, analysing human relationships and confronting some of the issues in an ever-changing world. As a writer who had in the past been able to pen material that appealed right across the board, the chances are that that material will still be in vogue whenever George decided to release it to the public.

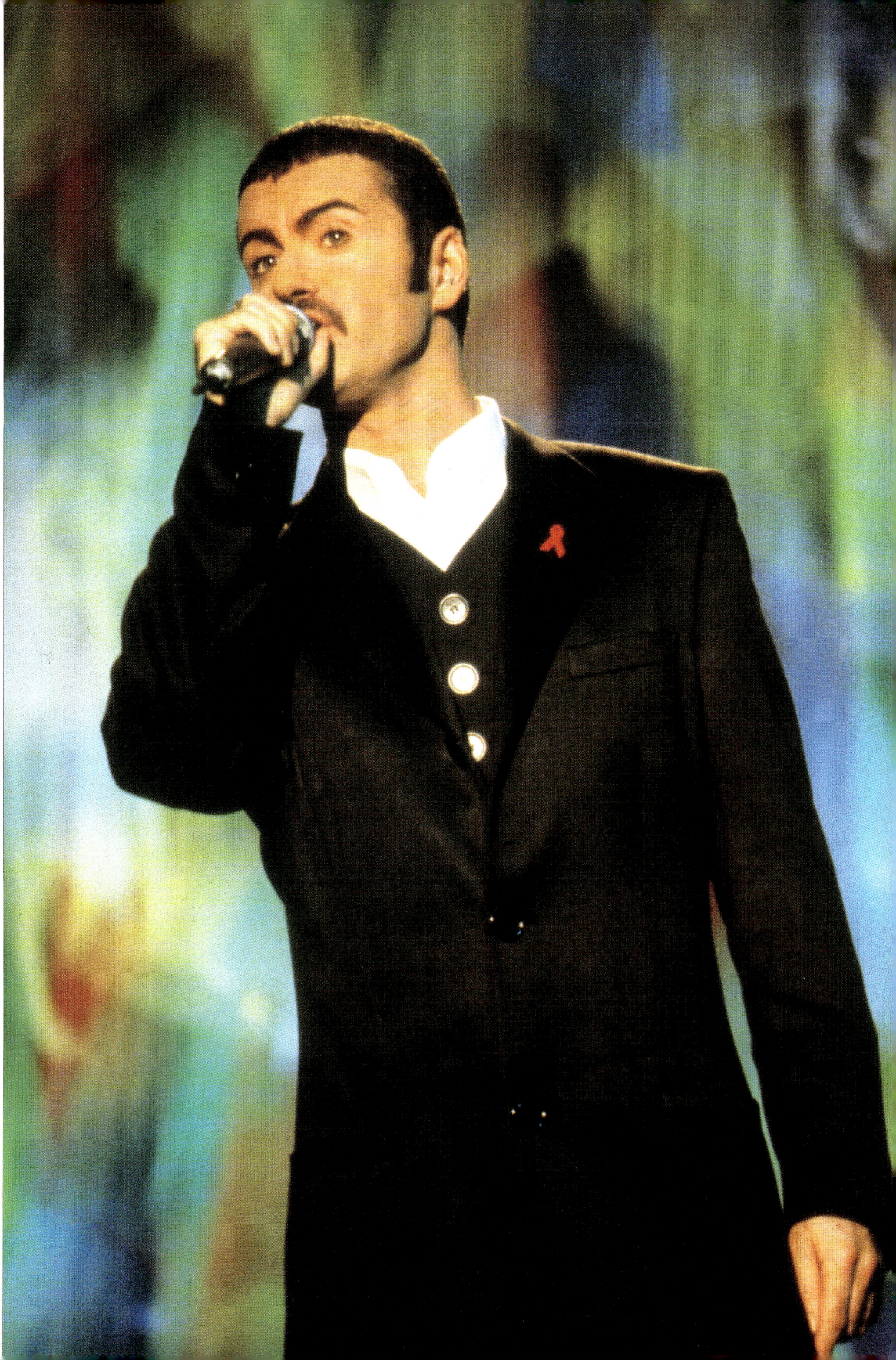

70 **GEORGE MICHAEL** READ WITHOUT PREJUDICE

While the court case revealed much about George Michael the artist, what about George Michael the man? 'I'm very analytical and pragmatic about myself,' he confessed. 'Sometimes I wish I were more instinctive but I put all the free aspects of my personality into my music. I'm probably far too old for my years but I'm glad I've grown up quickly because it means I can enjoy the rest of my life more. Growing up's not very enjoyable.

"When I came into this business," he continued, **"I really had no idea that I was going to be any kind of idol. I was a particularly unattractive adolescent and what made it worse was that my partner in Wham! Andrew Ridgeley was very handsome. I assumed that he would get most of the attention and that is what happened at first. Then things changed and I began to realise people didn't regard me as a Quasimodo. It was an odd feeling for someone who had been a fat boy with glasses who couldn't look at himself in the mirror. Suddenly there were all these girls who wanted to go to bed with me and I got carried away. I slept with an awful lot of them. I was making up for lost time because I didn't get much sex when I was a kid. Not many people were attracted to me and the ones that were were almost always ugly!"** George's early frankness over his sexuality was soon replaced by a more realistic view. The more the speculation grew, the more George chose to ignore it. **"I don't think people have the right to know whether I'm a spank freak, gay, bisexual, totally straight or celibate. I don't believe in knowing what people do in bed because I don't care what other people do in bed. I've got enough problems with what I do in bed."**

George took a similar stance over marriage. *"I'll only get married when I want to be a dad. Without a family I think marriage is a pointless exercise. And as far as I'm concerned I cannot afford to have kids until I've fulfiled my ambitions. It's no good being a part-time dad. I would want to be a full-time dad and not travelling all over the world promoting things. Marriage comes down to whether you love somebody enough. I don't know whether I've met that person. I have found it very difficult to share my own space with anybody. But eventually, it comes down to whether you love someone enough to sacrifice that space."*

"The things that get me down – like the lack of freedom or wanting to be in the right relationship or wanting an old relationship back – can only take up a certain amount of my energy these days, whereas they used to take up most of it." Speaking in 1990, George said *"Obviously the thing that's missing from my life is a stable relationship. But I don't wake up thinking I wish I was sharing my life with somebody, I've changed. Two or three years ago when I saw young guys in the park with their kids, I had this incredible sense of envy. It's gone. I don't know what's happened to it but it's gone. To me a successful relationship is where two people can live and exist happily together but still change and evolve."*

CHAPTER SEVEN **MOVING ON** 73

"My parents are in their fifties," he continued, *"and they've changed so much over the last ten years. A successful relationship is where the evolution of two people is allowed. But that's where people go wrong. They marry each other and are pretty much compatible, and then one of them goes off in one direction and the other either stays where they are or goes off in an opposing direction or they just can't accept changes...that's the greatest difficulty about people living together."* George said he couldn't imagine living with someone because his need for privacy was so much greater than most people's. *"When I was 19 or 20,"* he revealed, *"there were any number of fairly ordinary up to quite good-looking people I could take home. Now, if I chose to, I could walk into a room and leave with people who are much better looking or think a lot more of themselves. It's ironic really, now that I don't chose to, a lot of people are available to me. I find the idea of being that much of a catch for someone a very masculine and very castrating position to be in. There's no chase, you don't have to do anything."* Having spent the early part of his career, both with Wham! and as a solo performer, chasing stardom, George still felt there were times when he should be treated as an ordinary mortal. *"You have to be the type of person who can say no to everyone. When I go out I start with the intention, but everyone that comes up to you is different. I just can't give them a stock answer. With some people I feel bad about giving them the brush-off, but with others I take great pleasure in telling them to go away. I've got a set reply now for fans asking for autographs. I smile quite nicely and say 'Sorry, it's my night off' and it works – generally – because I'm friendly about it."*

One thing that had struck him was the fact that he was constantly met with smiles. **"Whenever I walk into a shop or see someone drive past in a car they're thinking, there's George Michael! I'll tell people about this tonight. I'll dine out on this one for a while. It's an experience. Therefore I get a very positive – although probably completely false – reaction from everyone I meet. You forget that that's not a normal experience and that most people are met with indifference. I'm never met with indifference. People always come towards me smiling."** In pursuing stardom, he concluded, he'd wasted a lot of time. He hadn't realised how meaningless chasing fame was until he'd taken it as far as he could. **"In the 1980s you didn't have to do much more than keep repeating what you had done and, as long as your youth was holding up and you weren't letting anybody down, you didn't have to worry much more than that."** George Michael certainly doesn't have to worry much any more – free to resume his recording career and just as successful as before his sabbatical. With two companies that were prepared to allow him the space to evolve as he thinks fit. That would release the singles he wanted in the order he wanted. And 1997 would find him back on the road, older, wiser and better.

In 1991, George claimed **"I don't feel the need to be a star any more."** But being a star is not a job or profession. It is the success that any artist enjoys (or endures!) that makes them a star. And the success George Michael has achieved has made him one of the true stars of the world of music. When George and Andrew set out on the road to stardom back in 1982, George's stated aim was to create songs that people would remember in 30 years time. Numbers like 'Wake Me Up Before You Go Go', 'Careless Whisper', 'Faith' and 'Jesus To A Child' are indicative of a talent that will undoubtedly attain that ambition.

Whatever the future may hold for George Michael as a singer, songwriter or man, he was already assured a certain immortality. A large percentage of the artists he and Andrew were battling with for chart glory in 1982 have long been confined to the memory banks. But George Michael just kept coming up with the goods.

Let George himself have the final word. **"I'm not an arrogant person. I don't think I'm particularly conceited, but I have a real inner confidence that this is what I was meant to do and that, whatever other failings I have, I am someone who has a craft, an ability, which has incredible by-products. Because of that, I never let situations get on top of me for any length of time. I really am an optimist and I believe that what I do is a good thing, a positive influence."**

Many millions of fans worldwide would agree.

76 **GEORGE MICHAEL** READ WITHOUT PREJUDICE

CHAPTER SEVEN **MOVING ON** 77

UK DISCOGRAPHY

WHAM!

SINGLES

'WHAM RAP (ENJOY WHAT YOU DO)'
Released June 1982 (reissued January 1983).
Highest chart position: 8.

'YOUNG GUNS (GO FOR IT)'
Released September 1982.
Highest chart position: 3.

'BAD BOYS'
Released May 1983.
Highest chart position: 2.

'CLUB TROPICANA'
Released July 1983.
Highest chart position: 4.

'CLUB FANTASTIC MEGAMIX'
Released November 1983.
Highest chart position: 15.

'WAKE ME UP BEFORE YOU GO GO'
Released May 1984.
Highest chart position: 1.

'FREEDOM'
Released October 1984.
Highest chart position: 1.

'LAST CHRISTMAS'
Released December 1984.
Highest chart position: 2.

'I'M YOUR MAN'
Released November 1985.
Highest chart position: 1.

'THE EDGE OF HEAVEN'
Released June 1986.
Highest chart position: 1.

ALBUMS

'FANTASTIC'
Bad Boys – A Ray Of Sunshine – Love Machine – Club Tropicana – Wham Rap (Enjoy What You Do) – Nothing Looks The Same In The Light – Young Guns (Go For It).
Released July 1983.
Highest chart position: 1.

'MAKE IT BIG'
Wake Me Up Before You Go Go – Everything She Wants – Like A Baby – Freedom – If You Were There – Credit Card Baby – Careless Whisper.
Released November 1984.
Highest chart position: 1.

'THE FINAL'
Wham Rap (Enjoy What You Do) – Young Guns (Go For It) – Bad Boys – Club Tropicana – Wake Me Up Before You Go Go – Where Did Your Heart Go – Careless Whisper – Freedom – Everything She Wants – Last Christmas – I'm Your Man – Battlestations – Blue (Armed With Love) – A Different Corner – The Edge Of Heaven.
Released October 1986.
Highest chart position: 1.

GEORGE MICHAEL

SINGLES

'CARELESS WHISPER'
Released July 1984.
Highest chart position: 1.

'A DIFFERENT CORNER'
Released March 1986.
Highest chart position: 1.

'I KNEW YOU WERE WAITING (FOR ME)'
with Aretha Franklin
Released January 1987.
Highest chart position: 1.

'I WANT YOUR SEX'
Released June 1987.
Highest chart position: 3.

'FAITH'
Released October 1987.
Highest chart position: 2

'FATHER FIGURE'
Released December 1987.
Highest chart position: 2.

'ONE MORE TRY'
Released April 1988.
Highest chart position: 8.

'MONKEY'
Released July 1988.
Highest chart position: 13.

'KISSING A FOOL'
Released November 1988.
Highest chart position: 18.

'PRAYING FOR TIME'
Released August 1990.
Highest chart position: 6.

'WAITING FOR THAT DAY'
Released October 1990.
Highest chart position: 23.

'FREEDOM '90'
Released December 1990.
Highest chart position: 28.

'HEAL THE PAIN'
Released February 1991.
Highest chart position: 31.

'COWBOYS AND ANGELS'
Released March 1991.
Highest chart position: 45.

'DON'T LET THE SUN GO DOWN ON ME'
with Elton John
Released November 1991.
Highest chart position: 1.

'TOO FUNKY'
Released June 1992.
Highest chart position: 4.

'FIVE LIVE EP'
with Queen and Lisa Stansfield
Somebody To Love – These Are The Days Of Our Lives – Calling You – Papa Was A Rolling Stone-Killer (Medley).
Released April 1993.
Highest chart position: 1.

'JESUS TO A CHILD'
Released January 1996.
Highest chart position: 1.

'FASTLOVE'
Released April 1996.
Highest chart position: 1.

'SPINNING THE WHEEL EP'
Spinning The Wheel - You Know That I Want To - Safe - Spinning The Wheel (Forthright Mix)
Released September 1996.
Highest chart position: 2.

ALBUMS

'FAITH'
Faith – Father Figure – I Want Your Sex (Pts 1 & 2) – Monkey – One More Try – Hand To Mouth – Look At Your Hands – Kissing A Fool.
Released November 1987.
Highest chart position: 1.

'LISTEN WITHOUT PREJUDICE Vol 1'
Praying For Time – Freedom '90 – They Won't Go When I Go – Something To Save – Cowboys And Angels – Waiting For That Day – Mother's Pride – Heal The Pain – Soul Free – Waiting (Reprise).
Released August 1990.
Highest chart position: 1.

'OLDER'
Jesus To A Child – Fastlove – Older – Spinning The Wheel – It Doesn't Really Matter – Strangest Thing – To Be Forgiven – Move On – Star People – You Have Been Loved – Free.
Released April 1996.
Highest chart position: 1.